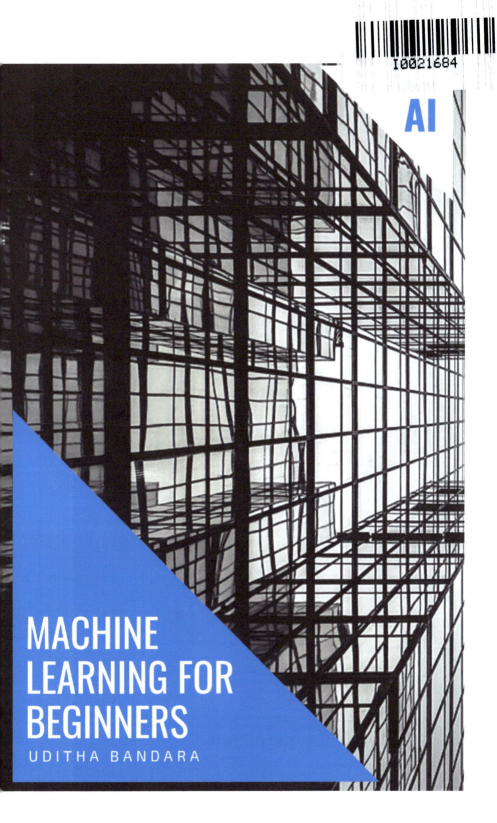

AI

MACHINE LEARNING FOR BEGINNERS

UDITHA BANDARA

Azure Machine Learning for beginners

Machine Learning for beginners

UDITHA BANDARA

ABOUT THE AUTHOR

UDITHA BANDARA (MVP) IS SPECIALIZES IN MICROSOFT DEVELOPMENT ,AI, MOBILE APP, CLOUD AND SOFTWARE TESTING TECHNOLOGIES. HE IS THE SOUTH EAST ASIA`S FIRST XNA/DIRECTX MVP (MOST VALUABLE PROFESSIONAL). HE HAD DELIVERED SESSIONS AT VARIOUS EVENTS AND CONFERENCES IN HONG KONG, MALAYSIA, SINGAPORE, CAMBODIA, INDONESIA, SRI LANKA AND INDIA. HE HAS PUBLISHED SEVERAL BOOKS,ARTICLES, TUTORIALS, AND DEMOS ON HIS BLOG – HTTPS://UDITHA.WORDPRESS.COM

DEDICATION

I would like to dedicate this book to my parents and my wife.

CONTENTS

1 INTRODUCTION TO AZURE AI & MACHINE LEARNING.

Azure is Microsoft cloud computing service. It provides various type of services for enterprise and consumers.

Fig 1.1

Application ,DevOps, Mobile, Database ,Analytics, Infra , security and many other services. In this book we are look into analytics and AI based services.
When it comes to Microsoft Azure AI technology stack it provides different set of services

Fig 1.2

Services ,Infrastructure and Tools are 3 main components of AI offering from Microsoft.

Azure Machine Leaning

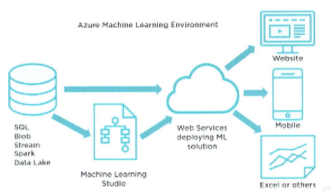

Fig 1.3

Azure Machine learning provide easy to build drag and drop UI environment. We can add data from different data sources and apply different data cleaning techniques. Cloud based environment helps to select appropriate algorithm and an deploy as standard web service.
We can select from different type of regression, Classification, clustering algorithm. If we cannot get selected algorithm it provides extendibility to implement in python or R.

Azure Cognitive services

Vision	Speech	Language	Knowledge	Search
• Computer Vision • Face • Content moderator • Video Indexer • Custom Vision*	• Speech to Text • Speaker Recognition* • Text to Speech • Speech Translation	• Text Analytics • Translator Text • Bing Spell Check • Language Understanding • Content Moderator	• QnA Maker	• Bing web • Bing Custom • Bing Visual • Bing Entity • Bing Video • Bing News • Bing ImageBing Autosuggest • Bing Local Business*

*In preview

Fig 1.4

Azure cognitive service provide pre-build AI models in computer Vision, Speech, Language , Knowledge and Search services. All these services are exposed as standard Json based web services. So it will be easy to integrate into any 3rd party non Microsoft platforms.
Fig 1.5 represent sample solution create using azure cognitive face detection service.

Fig 1.5

BOT Framework

Microsoft BOT Framework allows developer to crate intelligent bot application using different type of services such as email, skype, slack, SMS, telegram ,chat ,etc.

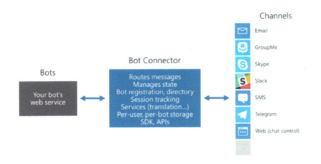

Fig 1.5

Using Microsoft Visual Studio developer can build intelligent bot applications. It can be integrate into standard web site, mobile app or other channels. **Fig 1.6 show BOT application based solution.**

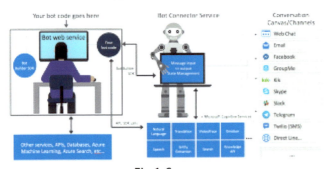

Fig 1.6

AI Compute

Azure Data Science Virtual Machine for Windows and Linux provide complete computing solution for data scientist. All major software tools and platforms pre-configured in this virtual machine.

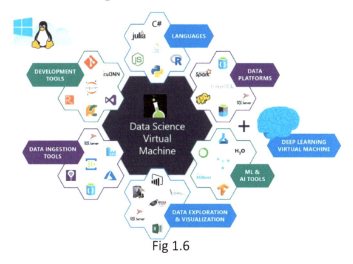

Fig 1.6

Installed software list-

Anaconda Python
R Server
Jupyter Notebooks
SQL Server
Python
Microsoft Cognitive Toolkit
Machine Learning Tools
Deep Learning Tools

2. REGRESSION

In statistical modeling, regression analysis is a set of statistical processes for estimating the relationships among variables.

$Y = a + bX$, where X is the explanatory variable and Y is the dependent variable. The slope of the line is b, and a is the intercept (the value of y when $x = 0$)

In regression we are going to look at vehicle price prediction algorithm. For this experiment we need past data on vehicle prices.

Fig 2.1

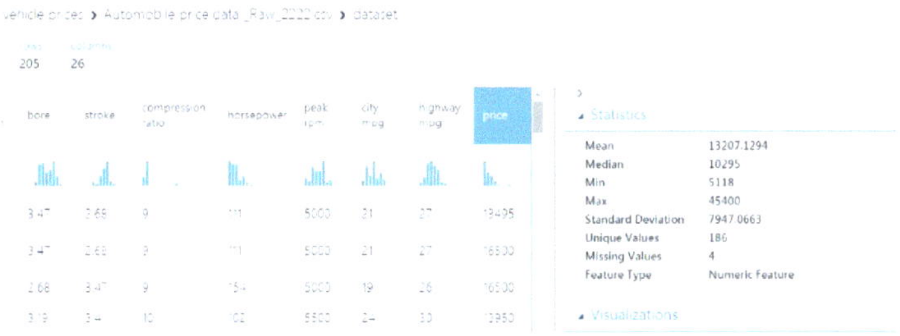

Fig 2.2

Vehicle price can be changed based on various reasons. Sometimes economic situation in those month matter to vehicle prices. In those cases you need to add economic factors into the consideration.

In our experiment we are looking at following data set for vehicle price predictions. Such as engine size, max torque, width, length etc. In those data set their might be unwanted data. Because raw data can come from various sources. It can come from different department from the organization such as accounting, marketing, finance ,operations etc.

But those data we gather might be unfit for the machine learning algorithm. So we need to clean those data to a point that it can used for the algorithm. Data cleaning need to be done carefully. It could takes few days to months to clean large dataset. But it's worth the effort other than getting false results from the machine learning algorithm.

In this data set ID is not necessary for the ml algorithm. ID values and codes are primarily used to identify unique product. But for machine learning algorithm such as regression It will be garbage. When cleaning raw data we also need to consider about missing values and null values. Because when you pass either missing or null values algorithm learns based on those false dataset.

So we need to either remove or update those data

based on median or mode values.

Azure machine Learning tool makes it easier to clean data. There are lot of options to clean data in azure machine learning. In order to clean data first we need to import the data set. We can add data using import wizard in azure machine learning.

Once you upload the data it will be available in our experiment. We can create new experiment in azure machine learning. Figure 2.1 shows that.

Once create a project we can give a name to the project. We can give Vehicle Price Prediction experiment.
Then under my dataset we can see vehicle price data. We can drag and drop into the surface.

Then we can right click and select visualize to see the raw dataset. First we can remove unwanted column by adding select column in dataset.

Fig 2.3

Fig 2.4

Then we can apply data cleaning techniques to original data set. here. For that we add clean missing data module.

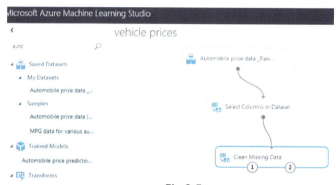

Fig 2.5

This module will go through all data and remove any missing data. Also we need to look at how much percentage of data missing in each column. Because if we have more percentage of missing data we end up removing more of our original data.

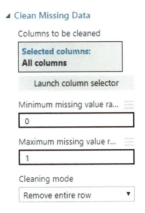

Fig 2.6

Now we are ready to select our feature set. We can use the following features(columns), which include the "price" feature that the model will attempt to predict:

- make
- body-style
- wheel-base
- engine-size
- horsepower
- peak-rpm
- highway-mpg
- price

vehicle prices

Fig 2.7

Fig 2.8

Afterward we can split data into two section. One is for training and other is for validating final result. Data can be split based in random selection. We can define percentage of split. In this project we are going to split 80% and 20%.

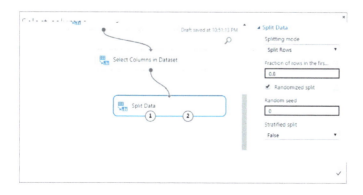

Fig 2.9

Now we are ready to apply appropriate algorithm for this project. Since we need to predict price of a vehicle this will be regression based project. We can start with basic regression algorithm , liner regression.

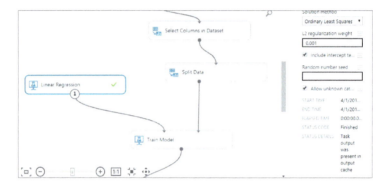

Fig 2.10

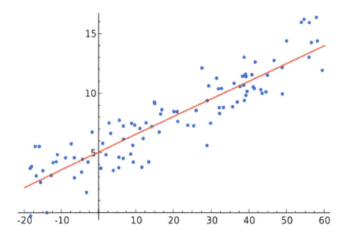

Fig 2.11

Liner regression is based on variation between two
variable. Training data needs to be fit into regression line.
Otherwise we can consider training is not successful. Also
we need to select price column for training.

Fig 2.12

Now we come to final stage of the project. Next we can
adding score module will provide training result. Also we
can add evaluate module to validate success of this project.

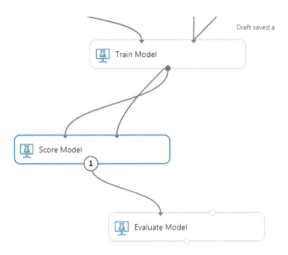

Fig 2.13

Score result will display learning prediction for price. And Evaluate module will display error and accuracy of the project . At least 89% or more needs to be archive to deploy as web service.

vehicle prices ❯ Score Model ❯ Scored dataset
vehicle prices ❯ Evaluate Model ❯ Evaluation results

▲ Metrics

Mean Absolute Error	1587.975994
Root Mean Squared Error	2502.355872
Relative Absolute Error	0.254917
Relative Squared Error	0.082756
Coefficient of Determination	0.917244

Fig 2.14
Fig 2.15

14

As a Data Scientist you have successfully build vehicle price predation project. Now it time to deploy this as a web service. Azure machine learning provides easy to use tools for web service deployment. More details about web services discussed in AML Web services chapter.

Fig 2.16

Fig 2.17

Fig 2.18

3 CLASSIFICATION

In this section we look at Classification using HR dataset. This can be used by HR manager of a company. Using churn based prediction we can predict next leaving employee.

Start a new experiment by clicking + NEW in the lower-left corner of the page, followed by Blank Experiment.

Fig 3.1

Creating a blank experiment

Click the default experiment name at the top of the canvas and change it to "HR Classification NH" (without quotation marks).

Fig 3.2

To see what this dataset looks like, click the output
port (the circle with the "1" in it) at the bottom of
the dataset and select Visualize.

Fig 3.3

The values in the dataset appear as columns, with
each row representing an employee data and each
column representing an employee feature. The far-
right column titled "left" is the target variable for
your predictive analysis. Scroll to the right until you
see this column. Then click it to select it.

You can view all statistics associate with each
column. In this project we are going to predict left to
be 0 or 1.

Next: Preprocess the data

No dataset is perfect. Most require some amount of preparation or cleaning before they can be used to train a model. When you visualized the data, you may have noticed that some rows were missing values. These need to be cleaned up before training begins.

> Connecting the dataset to the Select Columns in Dataset module

Fig 3.4

> Click the Select Columns in Dataset module on the experiment canvas to make sure it's selected, and then click the Launch column selector button in the Properties pane on the right.

It is time to build a model that uses a subset of the features in the dataset. You will use the following features (columns), which include the "left" feature that the model will attempt to predict:

Fig 3.5

- Satisfaction level
- Last evaluation
- Number of project
- Average monthly hours
- Time spend company
- Work accident
- left
- promotion_last_5years
- salary

Now it's time to remove rows containing blank values. Type "clean" (without quotation marks) into the search box at the top of the modules palette. Add a Clean Missing Data module to the experiment canvas and connect it to the output of the Select Columns in Dataset module. In the Properties pane, select Remove entire row from the list under cleaning mode to remove rows that have at least one missing value.

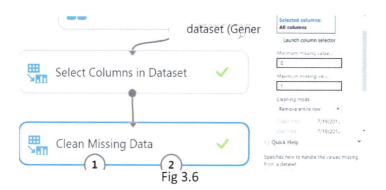

Fig 3.6

Double-click the Clean Missing Data module and enter the comment "Remove rows with missing values."

Next we can split data into two parts. One for training and other one for testing. For that we need to add spilt data module.

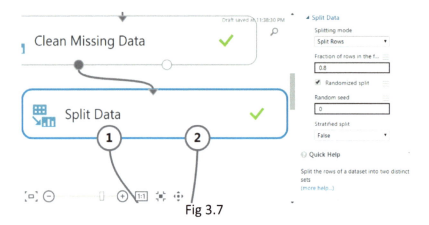

Fig 3.7

Now we can apply machine learning algorithm for this project. Since this is a classification problem we are going to use **two class boosted Decision tree** algorithm. This algorithm is a tree structure algorithm. It will go through decision tree to come with final predication.

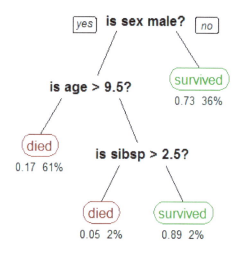

Fig 3.8

Fig 3.9

After that we can use both train and score modules to complete this project. Training module will connect to both algorithm and training data. In that we need to select training column. Afterward it can connect to score module.

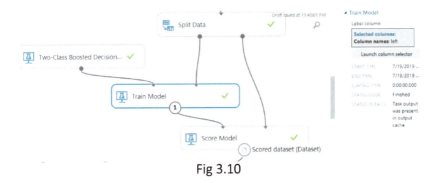

Fig 3.10

Score module contains learning predictions. We can match both original data and predicted data side by side. To get more accurate validation we can add evaluate module at the end.

Fig 3.11

Fig 3.12

Evaluate result contains accuracy of overall project. Accuracy of this project is 0.986. Also we can look at another four outputs. That is True Positive, False Positive, True Negative, and False Negative. On average True Positive needs to be higher than False Positive and True Negative needs to be higher than False Negative.

Fig 3.13

HR Classification NH

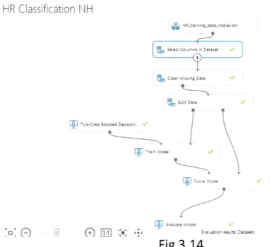

Fig 3.14

Complete Project.

After measuring success we can deploy this project as stranded web service. Azure machine learning built-in with web service features. We can connect to .NET app, excel, web page or mobile app (Android, IOS).

Fig 3.15

Training experiment | **Predictive experiment**

HR Classification NH [Predictive Exp.]

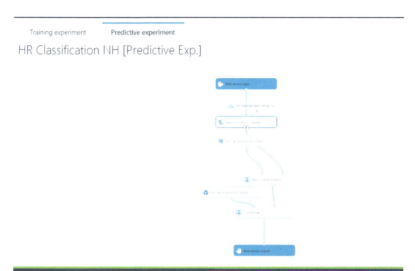

Fig 3.16

Fig 3.17

Fig 3.18

4 MATCHBOX RECOMMENDATIONS

In this section we look at product recommendation using IMDB Movie dataset. This can be used by e-commerce site to provide item recommendations.

Start a new experiment by clicking + NEW in the lower-left corner of the page, followed by Blank Experiment.

Fig 4.1

Creating a blank experiment

Click the default experiment name at the top of the canvas and change it to "Movie Recommendation NH" (without quotation marks). We need to add both movie rating and IMDB movie title datasets

Fig 4.2

Adding a dataset

To see what this dataset looks like, click the output port (the circle with the "1" in it) at the bottom of the dataset and select Visualize.

Fig 4.3

Rating data needs to be cast into integer format. We

can use Edit Metadata module for that.

Fig 4.4

In order to join both data sets we need to add Join data module with joining condition. Both data sets contains Movie ID value to join each other.

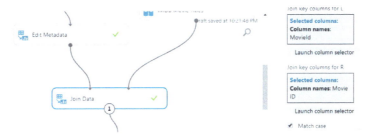

Fig 4.5

Next: Preprocess the data

No dataset is perfect. Most require some amount of preparation or cleaning before they can be used to train a model. When you visualized the data, you may have noticed that some rows were missing values. These need to be cleaned up before training begins.

Connecting the dataset to the Select Columns in Dataset module

Click the Select Columns in Dataset module on the experiment canvas to make sure it's selected, and then click the Launch column selector button in the Properties pane on the right.

Fig 4.6

Azure Machine Learning for beginners

It is time to build a model that uses a subset of the features in the dataset. You will use the following features (columns),

- User Id
- Movie Name
- Rating

In order to remove any duplicate data generated by joining we can use Remove Duplicate Rows module. Then select User Id and Movie Name.

Fig 4.7

Now we can spilt data into training and testing. For that we can apply Spilt data module with recommender split mode.

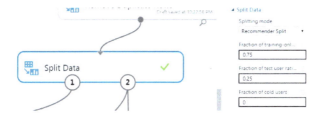

Fig 4.8

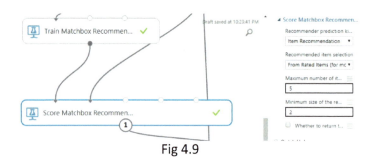

Fig 4.9

Afterward we can select algorithm for this project. Matchbox recommender is one of the algorithm we can use for this project. It was developed by Microsoft research. Then we can apply both score module and evaluate module to validate the result.

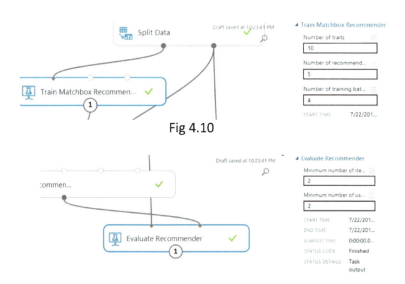

Fig 4.10

Fig 4.11

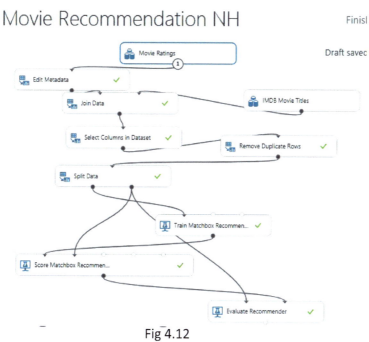

Fig 4.12

Complete Project.

Score module visualize recommendation for movies. After deploying as a web service we can use that to load relevant product items. Train module visualize overall successful percentage of this project.

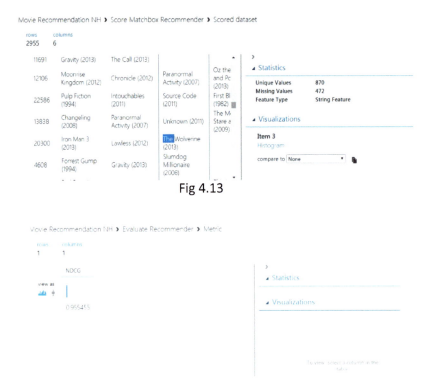

Fig 4.13

Movie Recommendation NH > Evaluate Recommender > Metric

rows   columns
1   1

        NDCG

view as
📊 ∔ |

        0.955455

        ‹   ›
        ◢ Statistics

        ◢ Visualizations

                        To view, select a column in the
                        table

Fig 4.14

5 AML WEB SERVICES

In this chapter we look at deploying data science project as a web service. Last part of the data science lifecycle project is to deploy as a mobile app or web site. Azure machine learning provides easy to use tools for that.

Data Science Lifecycle

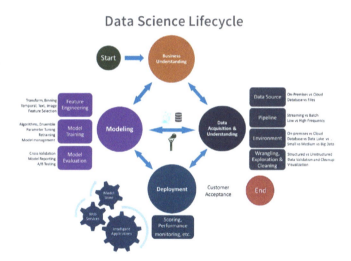

Fig 5.1

Once we select to generate web service project from machine learning project it will create separate web service environment. Then we can see separate web service API key to access.

Azure machine learning standard web service section provides API key with basic configurations. Also we can access basic test feature and excel template. In that we can select New Web Service Experience option to get more features.

Fig 5.2

Fig 5.3

Once that portal launched it will display several tabs. Quickstart tab display overall state and how-to documentation. Using that documentation developers can implement web site or desktop software to access web service.

Fig 5.4

Dashboard section will provide overall service calls. Also it will display errors in this service. Next we can navigate into Consume section. It will provide more in-depth sample code in C#, Python and R to access our web service. It also provide sample code to batch process. Using that we can make thousands of prediction at once. Another useful feature in this session is excel 2010 and 2013 templates. Using that we can make the perdition directly inside excel.

Fig 5.5

Fig 5.6

Fig 5.7

Fig 5.8

Azure ML Request – Response web app template provides build in web site for our web service. It will direct to Azure portal and generate web site. Azure also create domain to

publicly access this site. Next tab is testing section. That provides built in data to test machine learning project. We can also test machine learning project with new data in this section.

Fig 5.9

Fig 5.10

Last part of the web service tab is Swagger API. Using Swagger API we can use JSON based web service. Main advantage of using JSON based web service is that it can connect to any type of technology. Because JSON (JavaScript Object Notation) web service is platform independent. Using this we can connect our machine learning project with Android and Apple IOS mobile app. So users can download the app from the marketplace.

Fig 5.11

6 R & PYTHON INTEGRATION

Fig 6.1

In this chapter we look and integrating R and Python in Azure machine learning. Azure machine learning is not only drag and drop environment. It also provides high level of extendibility. If we look at any data science tool in the market it will be based on either R or Python. It hard to find one tool that support both language in one project. But in azure machine learning we can using both R and python along with drag and drop environment. So R developers , Python developer and beginner all can work in one project.

First we look at adding R language support for our project. Azure machine learning provide both open source R and Microsoft R in this environment .First we need to drag Execute R Script module in to the project.

Azure Machine Learning for beginners

Fig 6.2

Properties   Project

▲ Execute R Script

R Script

```
1  v <- version
2  property <- as.character(names(v))
3  value <- as.character(v)
4  data.set <- as.data.frame(cbind(property, value))
5  maml.mapOutputPort("data.set");
6
7
8  |
```

Fig 6.3

In this R code we will get R version and other system properties associate with the language. Once we run this script it will display R platform ,OS, System, Version and few other system information.

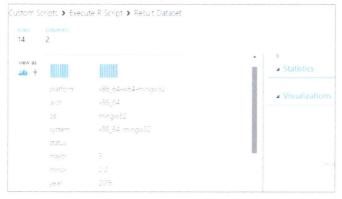

Fig 6.4

◢ Execute R Script

R Script

```
1 |
2 # Generate synthetic data
3 x <- seq(1, 30)
4 y <- x
5 noise <- runif(30, -1, 1)
6 ywnoise <- y + noise * 2
7
8 # plot point cloud on a chart
9 plot(x, ywnoise, xlab = NA, ylab = NA)
10
11 # combine two columns to create data grid
12 linoise <- cbind(x, ywnoise)
13 linoise <- as.data.frame(linoise)
14
15 # Select data.frame to be sent to the output Dataset port
16 maml.mapOutputPort("linoise");
```

Fig 6.5

In this R code we are generating random values from -1 to 1. And using built in plot function to generate the graph. We need to use maml.mapOutputPort() special method to return graph back to azure machine leaning environment.

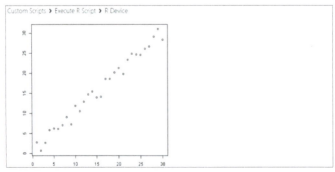

Fig 6.6

Python is really powerful programming language for data science and machine learning. Mastering python is really import to be an expert in machine learning . Next chapter we look more in-depth into python data science packages. In this module we look at adding python support to azure machine learning. We can select between two different python versions. Both are running on Anaconda runtime. Anaconda runtime is a standard environment for python data science and machine leaning.

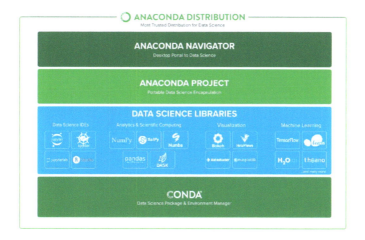

Fig 6.7

Fig 6.8

First we can add Execute python script module to implement python code. In this code we look at python language version and system information. In Azure machine learning we need to use special build in **azureml_main()** python function. We can import up to three different datasets. Finally data need to return back to azure machine learning environment. In this code we are using **return df** for that.

▲ Execute Python Script

Python script

```
1 import pandas as pd
2 import sys
3 def azureml_main(dataframe1 = None, dataframe2 = None):
4     prop = ['major', 'minor', 'micro', 'releaselevel', 'serial']
5     val = sys.version_info[:]
6     d = {"prop" : prop, "val" : [str(v) for v in val]}
7     df = pd.DataFrame(d)
8     return df,
9
```

Fig 6.9

48

Fig 6.10

In next code we are going to generate random data and display in a graph. For that we need to import several packages. Numpy and Pandas are two major packages for data processing and manipulations. Also we need to import matplotlib package to display our graph. Once we setup X and Y , we can use plot() to display graph. In Azure machine leaning we need to save graph in to image format and return back to the environment.

```
Python script

1  import matplotlib
2  matplotlib.use('agg')
3  import numpy as np
4  import matplotlib.pyplot as plt
5  import pandas as pd
6  def azureml_main(dataframe1=None, dataframe2=None):
7      x = range(1, 31)
8      y = x
9      noise = np.random.uniform(-1, 1, 30)
10     ywnoise = y + noise * 2
11
12     d = {'x' : np.asarray(x), 'ywnoise' : ywnoise}
13     linoise = pd.DataFrame(d)
14
15     fig = plt.figure()
16     ax = fig.gca()
17     linoise.plot(kind='line', ax=ax, x='x', y='ywnoise')
18     fig.savefig('linoise.png')
19     return linoise
```

Fig 6.11

Custom Scripts > Execute Python Script > Python device

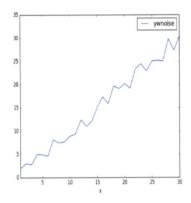

Fig 6.12

7 PYTHON CLOUD NOTEBOOK

Azure machine learning comes built in with Jupyter notebook software. It helps data scientist to implement code in more visually supporting environment. In Azure machine learning we do not need to worry about computing. All the processing runs on cloud. We can select from Python 2,3 or R. Once we select python 3 it ask for notebook name.

Fig 7.1

Fig 7.2

Jupyter notebook runs in cell based environment. We can put individual code block in each cell. Cell can execute separately. Also we can export code as .py or .pdf formats. Azure machine learning provides auto save feature for the code.

Fig 7.3

```
In [1]: import numpy as np
        a = np.array([1,2,3], float)
        b = np.array([5,2,6], float)
        print(a)
        print(b)


        [ 1.  2.  3.]
        [ 5.  2.  6.]
```

Fig 7.4

First we import Numpy data science packages in this code. It comes build in with basics set of data structures and mathematical functions. In this code we are creating two arrays called a and b. Then we are using print function to see the result.

```
In [2]: print(a + b)
        print(a - b)
        print(a * b)
        print(b / a)


        [ 6.  4.  9.]
        [-4.  0. -3.]
        [ 5.  4. 18.]
        [ 5.  1.  2.]
```

Fig 7.5

In this python code we are implementing basic calculation for a and b Numpy arrays. We are implementing addition, subtraction, multiplication and division.

```
In [3]: basic_list = [14, 7, 15, 7, 3, 5, 6, 8, 10]

        print("length: ", len(basic_list))
        print("min: ", min(basic_list))
        print("max: ", max(basic_list))

        length:  9
        min:  3
        max:  15
```

Fig 7.6

In this code we are creating basic Numpy list and using built-in features for calculate length, minimum and maximum.

```
In [15]: import pandas as pd

         df = pd.DataFrame({'A': ['foo', 'bar', 'foo', 'bar',
                                  'foo', 'bar', 'foo', 'foo'],
                            'B': ['one', 'one', 'two', 'three',
                                  'two', 'two', 'one', 'three'],
                            'C': np.random.randn(8),
                            'D': np.random.randn(8)})

         print(df)

              A      B         C         D
         0  foo    one  1.093086 -0.391003
         1  bar    one -1.376710 -0.776302
         2  foo    two  0.218171 -0.317017
         3  bar  three -2.191496  0.023307
         4  foo    two  0.901524  0.551573
         5  bar    two  1.915389  1.462126
         6  foo    one  0.985522  1.346589
         7  foo  three  0.192946 -0.376150
```

Fig 7.7

Next we can add Pandas data science package. This

package is mainly used for data processing. One of the main feature of this package is handling of rows and columns using data frame. In this code we are having A,B,C,D column with 8 rows. A and B contains text based data.
C and D contains random generated data.

```
In [7]: import numpy as np
        import matplotlib.pyplot as plt

        objects = ('Python', 'C++', 'Java', 'Perl', 'Scala', 'Lisp')
        y_pos = np.arange(len(objects))
        performance = [10,8,6,4,2,1]

        plt.bar(y_pos, performance, align='center', alpha=0.5)
        plt.xticks(y_pos, objects)
        plt.ylabel('Usage')
        plt.title('Programming language usage')


        plt.show()
```

Fig 7.8

In this code we are using popular plotting library Matplotlib. First we are creating bar chart. Bar objects are Python, C++, Java, Perl, Scala and Lisp. Then we are giving height value for each object. We can add more details by adding title, ylable addition functions.

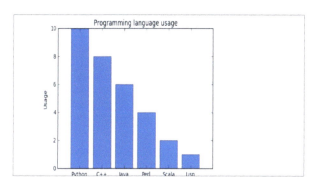

Fig 7.9

```
In [10]: import matplotlib.pyplot as plt

         labels = 'Frogs', 'Hogs', 'Dogs', 'Logs'
         sizes  = [15, 30, 45, 10]
         explode = (0, 0.0, 0, 0.2)


         fig1, ax1 = plt.subplots()
         ax1.pie(sizes, explode=explode, labels=labels, autopct='%1.1f%%',
                 shadow=True, startangle=90)
         ax1.axis('equal')

         plt.show()
```

Fig 7.10

Next type of chart is pie chart. We can define pie objects first. Then percentage for each items. By using pie() function we can provide all the basics configuration for this chart.

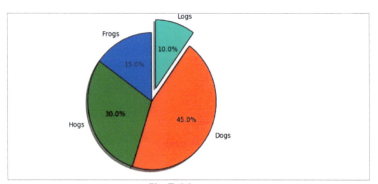

Fig 7.11

```
In [11]: import numpy as np
         import matplotlib.pyplot as plt

         # Fixing random state for reproducibility
         np.random.seed(19680801)

         # Compute areas and colors
         N = 150
         r = 2 * np.random.rand(N)
         theta = 2 * np.pi * np.random.rand(N)
         area = 200 * r**2
         colors = theta

         fig = plt.figure()
         ax = fig.add_subplot(111, projection='polar')
         c = ax.scatter(theta, r, c=colors, s=area, cmap='hsv', alpha=0.75)
         plt.show()
```

Fig 7.12

Last type of chart in this chapter is scatter plot. We can generate random data to display in this chart. By defining N, r, theta, area and colors we can call scatter () function.

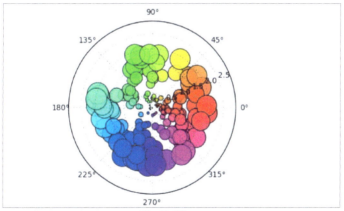

Fig 7.13

Azure Machine Learning for beginners

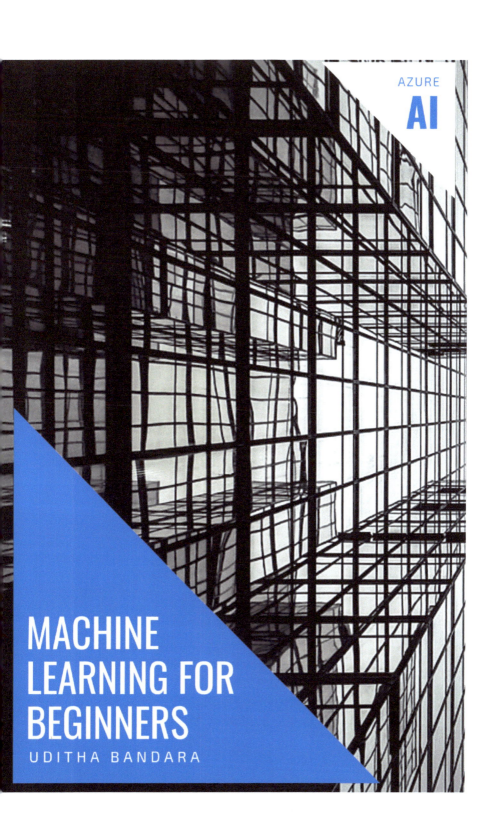

AZURE

AI

MACHINE
LEARNING FOR
BEGINNERS

UDITHA BANDARA

www.ingramcontent.com/pod-product-compliance
Lightning Source LLC
Chambersburg PA
CBHW041155050326
40690CB00004B/568